30-Day Journey

with Julian of Norwich

W0009845

30-Day Journey

with Julian of Norwich

Compiled and Edited by Carol Howard Merritt

Broadleaf Books

Minneapolis

30-DAY JOURNEY WITH JULIAN OF NORWICH

Print ISBN: 978-1-5064-6442-8
eBook ISBN: 978-1-5064-6443-5

Cover design: Paul Soupiset
Interior design: Paul Soupiset
Typesetting: Jessica Ess, Hillspring Books

Excerpts from Julian of Norwich, *Showings*, translated and introduced by Edmund Colledge, OSA, and James Walsh, SJ, copyright
© 1978 by Paulist Press, Inc., New York/Mahwah, NJ. Reprinted
by permission of Paulist Press, Inc. www.paulistpress.com.

Contents

"He is our clothing,
for he is that love which
wraps us and enfolds us,
embraces us and guides us,
surrounds us for his love,
which is so tender that he
may never desert us."

—Julian of Norwich

Introduction

Dear Friend,

I open my inbox to discover a rejection letter from a church. It greets me like a punch in the gut. My contract at my current position will end soon, so I am scurrying to find another one. I serve as a transitional pastor, which means I spent most of my chaotic year packing, unpacking, and packing again. And now I am sorting through a series of options, feeling uncertain about my call, knowing that I would love to do God's will, if I only knew what it looks like. Of course, the trials of a job search pale in comparison to the pandemic that looms—in the news, on surfaces, and even in the air particles surrounding me. Older friends have died alone, a pregnancy ended with a stillbirth, and my teeth feel on edge with constant anxiety when I contemplate what other horrors might be ahead.

In short, my soul desperately needs to hear the words, "All shall be well." Each morning throughout this tumultuous storm, Julian of Norwich anchors me in the truth of God's love and care. Her visions have come as a balm, soothing this scourging suffering with God's goodness and love.

As you work through the next thirty days of passages, you might want to grab a journal or notebook and spend some time answering the questions at the end of each entry. For I have found that Julian's words are not a dip in a shallow pool, but a deep dive. They become most powerful when we can wrestle with them and apply them. I pray that you will feel that same peace as you journey with Julian.

Carol Howard Merritt
July 2020

Days 1–30

Julian Asks for Suffering

I desired three graces by the gift of God. The first was to have recollection of Christ's passion. The second was a bodily sickness, and the third was to have, of God's gift, three wounds.

Julian of Norwich was a child during the height of the bubonic plague in Europe. The black death wiped out a quarter of the population. With so much suffering surrounding her, I wonder why she craved the depths of human experience. I construct my life to avoid pain. When I notice the slightest headache creeping into the back of my eyes, I reach for the aspirin and pray the discomfort will dissolve along with the pill. I ask God to take misery away, instead of increasing it. Julian, on the other hand, believed that the adversity would lead her to a bond with Jesus and those who love him.

While I don't desire hardship, I do recognize its strange power. When I meet someone who knows a pain similar to one I've endured, a peculiar solidarity blossoms. They can see the vulnerable parts I have tried to cover with some sort of mask. A connection grows through the shared heartache of betrayal or loss. Then I turn back to Julian, realizing that when we feel pain within ourselves, we can recognize suffering in others.

For Reflection

Where is the pain in your life? Is there someone you know who shares that suffering? Can you reach out to them or pray for them?

Contrition, Compassion, and Longing

I conceived a great desire, and prayed our Lord God that he would grant me in the course of my life three wounds, that is, the wound of contrition, the wound of compassion, and the wound of longing with my will for God.

Neurologists are working on a pill that can wipe out the memories of traumatic experiences. The possibility terrifies me. Without the memory of suffering, how would we know that we have done something wrong? When we touch an open flame, the pain tells us that we must avoid the heat in the future. In the same way, when we wound another person, our burning regret reminds us to refrain from that action in the future.

Julian knew that we needed the wound of contrition. If we could swallow a pill to wipe out our memories, we would not feel the weight of the things we did wrong. We could no longer sense heartache in others. We could not catch a glimpse of what Christ saw when he suffered the depths of human pain with us.

For Reflection

Write down an action that you regret. Take three deep breaths while remembering the pain you caused in yourself or in another person. Take three more breaths. This time, as you exhale, think of letting go of that pain or remorse. Take three more breaths while imagining God holding you and loving you in your pain.

Passion and Compassion

And suddenly it came into my mind that I ought to wish for the second wound, that our Lord, of his gift and of his grace, would fill my body full with recollection and feeling of his blessed passion, as I had prayed before, for I wished that his pains might be my pains, with compassion which would lead to longing for God.

While I don't understand Julian's desire for pain, I do know that I cannot avoid pain in life. When I'm going through it, I yearn to attach some meaning to it. I cannot help but ask, *Why? Why must I go through this experience? Is there anything that I can learn from it?*

Julian found a longing for God in the midst of her pain. Likewise, as I think of times when a prayer constantly hung on my lips, when God felt as close as my breath, I know they took place when I suffered agony, rejection, or loss of a loved one. Moments of divine yearning occur when I walk in the midst of suffering. Misery can produce a raw loneliness. I feel like I can't expose my vulnerable heart to another human, so no one can understand its throbbing bruise. And so, I long for God and hope that the answer to my *why* will be revealed. In God, I am not alone in the heartache.

For Reflection

Remember a time when you felt particularly near to God. What was happening in your life? Is there a connection between your pain and your longing for God?

Familiar Love

I saw that he is to us everything which is good and comforting for our help. He is our clothing, for he is that love which wraps us and enfolds us, embraces us and guides us, surrounds us for his love, which is so tender that he may never desert us.

As we develop, humans need certain things, like food, water, and shelter. Then we have other necessities that often go unfulfilled. We need tenderness to surround us. We need a sense of belonging. We need to know that no matter how many mistakes we make, we will be loved. Unfortunately, we are all imperfect humans, including our parents. Some parents could not be present. Others could not give us the love we needed. We might have received a transactional affection based on our performance, success, or ability to obey. Or love might have been withheld completely. As a result, we developed into these messy humans who take a lifetime trying to love well.

In the midst of these disappointments with others and ourselves, Julian's words soothe us, reminding us that even when our imperfect human love proves unreliable, God surrounds us with a love that is so comforting, it's like a sweater, wrapping us in warmth and comfort.

For Reflection

Find your softest blanket. Wrap it around yourself and close your eyes. Meditate on God's love surrounding you and giving you that unconditional love. Though this world can be dark and cold, may God waken us to the love that always embraces us.

Hazelnut

And in this he showed me something small, no bigger than a hazelnut, lying in the palm of my hand, and I perceived that it was round as any ball. I looked at it and thought: What can this be? And I was given this general answer: It is everything which is made.

Throughout history, visionaries have imparted a unique perspective. Like Georgia O'Keeffe with a paintbrush and flower, we can zoom into our subject, seeing the minute details. We perceive things that we would have missed—the texture of a petal or the form of the stigma.

Or we see the perspective of Mary Cassatt, viewing the horizon. The beauty of a poppy field startles us as we focus on that place where the sky and earth kiss.

In the mid-twentieth century, we understood a completely different perspective when we received the first images of Earth taken from space. We could see the world as a swirly marble.

Of course, Julian of Norwich caught a vision of that spherical earth one hundred fifty years before Galileo's telescope or Magellan's journey became instrumental in proving its existence, for God gave her that perspective with the hazelnut. As she held the small seed in the palm of her hand, she understood that it contained the world. In that moment, she saw with God's perspective.

For Reflection

Find something you can hold in the palm of your hand—a ball, marble, or nut. Now, think about all of the challenges you will face today. How big are they, from this perspective?

God Made, Loves, and Preserves It

In this little thing I saw three properties. The first is that God made it, the second is that he loves it, the third is that God preserves it.

George Washington Carver asked God for the secrets of the universe. And God answered: "I will give you the secrets of the peanut." Then Carver created three hundred products by exploring the complexities of that small seed.

In much the same way, Julian understood the nature of God and creation by contemplating a hazelnut. God made the world, just as God made the seed, and that tiny nut has the potential to become a tree with an incredible hardiness that can stand for eight thousand years, producing sustenance as it does. In the palm of her hand Julian saw God's love, compact and emanating. What else but love can create such a marvel?

Just as Jesus wondered over the mustard seed and Carver pondered the peanut, Julian saw the hazelnut. Through their eyes, we understand that in creation, something that can fit into the palm of our hand can be a world unto itself.

For Reflection

Notice something or someone in your life that has great potential. It may be a seed, a child, or a talent. What is one thing you can do today to nurture that person or thing?

Perspective

But the reason why it seemed to my eyes so little was because I saw it in the presence of him who is the Creator.

When I read about a historical event, I find that it becomes difficult to digest large numbers. When I see a staggering tally of deaths while reading about a war or pandemic, I focus on singular lives, trying to hold on to the fact that each number was a part of a network of family, friends, and loved ones. The truth of history seems to exist between the microscope and the telescope.

I wonder if Julian felt the same way as the plague hit her village and a fourth of the people she knew died. Yet, she stood there, looking at the hazelnut, with God whispering in her ear, telling her that it was the universe. Somehow, Julian was able to back away from her suffering body, her priory room, and the roads filled with corpses, and understand the world as God sees it. While Julian felt the intensity of the suffering of one human life, she was also able to understand the planet and creation in a way that still strikes us today. For she could perceive that contained in that tiny nut was everything it needed for sustenance. In that seed, she sensed God's love and care flowing from something that fit in the palm of her hand.

For Reflection

What historic event has touched your life or the lives of your family? Can you name a way that you have been able to gain perspective from that situation?

Cutting Yourself Off from Love

God is everything that is good, and God has made everything that is made, and God loves everything that he has made, and if any man or woman withdraws his love from any of his fellow Christians, he does not love at all, because he has not love towards all.

Ghosting: I learned the skill at an early age, before the noun morphed into a verb. I avoided people who hurt me, cutting them off before they could wound me again. While this act of self-preservation made sense as a youth, when I got older and stronger, I kept the habit. Instead of telling people when they had harmed me with a slight or a stinging word, I withdrew my love until I felt isolated, with a long list of former friends.

When we get involved with the messiness of one another's lives, we push on tender spots. Pain always attends with deep love. The aching pulses with thoughtless words, lashing out, or rejection, but unless abuse occurs, we must learn to connect through it.

Julian knew that if we cut one another off, we become isolated from our community and closed off from God. For God's love uses the channels of humanity to flow to us and through us. When we dam every connection, we can no longer receive love.

For Reflection

Whom have you cut off? Do you need to make amends with someone? Write down their name. Can you take one small step toward connection?

The Goodness of God

But because I am a woman, ought I therefore to believe that I should not tell you of the goodness of God, when I saw at that same time that it is his will that it be known?

Julian of Norwich wrote down her visions in a cloistered room. For hundreds of years, women took Julian's words, treasured them, and preserved them, until they emerged from the monastery walls with astounding resonance.

Historic norms direct that women should not have a voice when speaking of God. Most of Christianity cuts women off from leading roles, either by explicitly declaring that women's leadership is unorthodox or by constantly overlooking women when calling preachers to fill their pulpits.

Yet, voices like Julian's persist in telling the goodness of God. Women moved from the empty tomb to inform the other disciples what they had seen. Women teach their children the stories that form them. And women write theology from cloistered rooms so that we might read it, treasure it, and preserve it. Throughout history, the voices of women have broken through cultural constraints in order to speak of God's goodness.

Why? It is because of the simple truth that Julian lays bare: God wills it. And when it comes to God's will, no patriarchy can crush it, no ecclesial body can silence it. Even if it takes a hundred or a thousand years, we cannot deter God's will.

For Reflection

What is God's will for you? Is there something you should be doing, but our cultural constraints hold you back?

Sport, Scorn, Seriousness

I see sport, that the devil is overcome; and I see scorn, that God scorns him and he will be scorned; and I see seriousness, that he is overcome by the passion of our Lord Jesus Christ and by his death, which was accomplished in great earnest with heavy labor.

Throughout Christian history, theologians have sought to understand what happened on the cross. Some speak of Christ's death as the perfect sacrifice to satisfy a payment for our sins. Others see the suffering as a chance for Christ to vindicate God's honor. Still others see the cross as a tool on which Christ becomes victorious over death, through the resurrection.

Julian compares Jesus's death with laboring, as a mother giving birth. As she contemplates Christ's death on the cross, she equates it with the pain of contractions and a dilating cervix. For just as a mother labors for a new creation in an extraordinary and painful act of love, Jesus suffers in order to accomplish the work of salvation and our abundant life. When we turn to the outpouring of Christ's love, salvation has been accomplished.

For Reflection

Hold a cross in your hand or look at one. Is there a word that comes to your mind when you remember how Jesus suffered? Meditate on that word.

In Sorrow as in Joy

God wishes us to know that he keeps us safe all the time, in joy and in sorrow, and that he loves us as much in sorrow as in joy.

Bob looks at his crossword puzzle and tries to figure out the words before him. The word games are pretty much all he can do as he recovers from his heart surgery. As he tries to make the letters fit into the tiny boxes, he struggles with a much bigger puzzle in his mind. He wonders, *Why did God cause my suffering?*

Bob is not alone in his soul-searching. We often want to find meaning behind suffering, and in doing so, we might wonder if God is punishing us. Or if God quit loving us. Did we do something to deserve God's wrath? Is this God's judgment? Or is it a lesson that God is forcing us to learn through hardship?

Julian reminds us that God's love extends in our pain and our comfort, in our hardships and our ease. That outpouring of love does not stop when we suffer. It always surrounds us.

For Reflection

Light a candle. When have you lit a candle in the past? Was it to celebrate a birthday or dispel the darkness of a storm? Were you gathering in protest? Were you praying for a dying loved one? Think of that flame as God's love attending you, in sorrow and in celebration.

Solidarity

And here I saw a great unity between Christ and us; for when he was in pain we were in pain, and all creatures able to suffer pain suffered with him.

After years of praying for a child, Maria had a miscarriage. She clenched her fist against the unbearable grief and stabbing pains in her gut as she prayed the only muttering that she could muster: "God, where are you?"

In our human weakness, we may want a God who will come on the scene like a fairy godmother and swoosh her magical baton until everything terrible goes away. And yet, the truth of God's goodness is so much more complicated than that. For God offers us solidarity in Jesus Christ. There is no animated erasure, but rather a deep understanding of our gut-wrenching tears. Our God sits with us in our pain and bears our sorrows. With the strength of vulnerability, God suffers with us.

For Reflection

Think about a time when you were in pain. It could be a physical, emotional, or mental suffering. Now imagine God in the room with you. What is God feeling? How is God responding?

Suffering and Love

But the love which made him suffer all this surpasses all his pains as far as heaven is above the earth. For his pains were a deed, performed once through the motion of love; but his love was without beginning and is and ever will be without any end.

When my daughter was a child and she would get hurt, I would see the tears welling up and all of my instincts told me to shush her. I wanted to tell her that the pain wasn't that bad, that she should toughen up, or that she should deny her suffering in some way. But I knew that sometimes we just have to go through the anguish. So, I sat with my tiny child, hugged her, and kissed the top of her head as I reminded myself: joy comes in the morning.

Whether I feel devastated or I feel the pain of a loved one, I must tell myself that the tears will end. The bruise will fade, the wound will scar, and that acute pang will diminish. And yet, when two people share the vulnerability of pain and heartache, a bond remains after the tears have dried.

In Julian's visions, she reminds us that pain is temporary, but love is eternal. Though grief and heartache fade, the love remains.

For Reflection

If you are able, throw a rock into a body of water. (If you can't, then imagine the act.) The rock touching the surface is the pain. The water is God's love. Notice how the splash and ripple last for a moment, but they do not affect the larger body. Love remains.

What Is Sin?

In the word "sin," our Lord brought generally to my mind all which is not good: the shameful contempt and the complete denial of himself which he endured for us in this life and in his death, and all the pains and passions, spiritual and bodily, of all his creatures.

In Jay's childhood church, pastors often railed against the sin of drinking. Then, as Jay got older, he developed severe anxiety, which he learned to manage with alcohol. Finally, Jay realized he was an alcoholic.

Jay began to berate himself, hoping to kick the habit. He reached back to those messages of his youth: he was a sinful wretch and God was angry at him for drinking. The messages never worked. He simply got trapped in a quagmire of shame.

Through a twelve-step program, Jay met a group of friends who lived with dual diagnoses, and he began to understand his relationship to the drug. As a young man, before he understood his anxiety, he needed alcohol to survive difficult situations. As he got older and sought the medication he required, Jay began to recover.

When Jay scolded himself for the addiction, he could not overcome it. Yet, when he began to understand it as something that had been necessary at one point, but eventually led to destruction in his life, he felt compassion on himself and learned to seek a deeper understanding.

For Reflection

Think of an action in your past that makes you feel guilty. Were you angry? Were you jealous? Did you lie or lash out at someone? Think about the first time you had that reaction. Was it as a child? Did you react in that way to protect yourself? Can you forgive yourself?

Sin Has No Substance

But I did not see sin, for I believe that it has no kind of substance, no share in being, nor can it be recognized except by the pain which it causes.

As a young woman, I attended a fundamentalist Bible college. Upon admittance, in the mail I received a one-inch-thick rulebook, guidelines for our student life together. I flipped through the book and realized that the school had tried to name every possible thing we could do wrong, and then they had added anything that could cause temptation. There were prohibitions about everything, from facial hair to open-toed shoes.

This is what happens when we try to give sin a substance—we end up with a giant list of rules that could never encompass the myriad ways we can offend one another.

Julian, in contrast, does not look at the substance of sin, but at the effects. Sin is that which causes pain—the heartache of betrayal, the suffering of cruelty, or the anguish of greed.

For Reflection

Is there some time in your life when you caused grief or heartache? Write down a word that symbolizes that moment. Did you try to justify your action because it wasn't that bad? Can you recognize it as wrong by the pain it caused? Can you receive God's mercy and love? Now destroy that paper. Burn it or tear it up. In some way let it go, as you receive God's forgiveness.

Christ Has Compassion on Us Because of Sin

So it would be most unkind of me to blame God or marvel at him on account of my sins, since he does not blame me for sins. So I saw how Christ has compassion on us because of sin; and just as I was before full of pain and compassion on account of Christ's passion, so I was now in measure filled with compassion for all my fellow Christians, and then I saw that every kind of compassion which one has for one's fellow Christians in love is Christ in us.

Judy often lost her temper at her son. The red-hot fury flared at the slightest provocation. She knew that her anger had much more to do with her own exhaustion and stress than it did with her child's behavior. And when the ferocious fires died down, Judy's anger turned inward as she berated herself for her bad behavior.

This cycle continued—the flames of anger would turn into the embers of remorse. Judy would beg her son for forgiveness. Everything would settle, until something ignited the rage again.

The sequence of events continued until Judy learned to have compassion. She remembered when she was a child and fear would rise up when her mother became angry with her. Instead of feeling guilt, she began to have empathy with that little girl. She began to understand the love that God had for her. When she learned to have tenderness toward herself, she could practice it toward her child. Eventually, the practice of compassion overtook the cycle of fury and self-hatred.

For Reflection

Is there a time in your life when you began to understand Christ's compassion toward you and, in turn, felt more compassion toward others?

All Shall Be Well

And so our good Lord answered to all the questions and doubts which I could raise, saying most comfortingly in this fashion: I will make all things well, I shall make all things well, I may make all things well, and I can make all things well; and you will see that yourself, that all things will be well.

I imagine Julian, cloistered in Norwich after the plague had ravaged the town. She watched from her tower and remembered how the foul stench of death and mourning rose up from the streets. In the midst of such heartache, she continued to question and doubt. And God assured her that all things would be made well.

Julian didn't stop questioning, nor did she walk away from the pain that surrounded her. She did not deny it, but rather she trudged through the valley of the shadow of death and came out knowing the goodness of God and that all would be well.

And those words that she heard, that she transmitted to us, continue to comfort our souls in the midst of our own fear and trembling: *All shall be well.*

For Reflection

Take seven deep breaths while meditating on the words "All shall be well."

Christ's Spiritual Thirst

For his spiritual thirst is his longing in love, and that persists and always will until we see him on the day of judgment, for we who shall be saved and shall be Christ's joy and bliss are still here, and shall be until that day.

I think of that moment when Christ hangs on the cross and says, "I thirst." Exposing complete vulnerability, Jesus announces his human need and weakness. As the stories of that afternoon echo through the centuries, we know that we have a God who suffers with us. In that crucified body, we do not have a watchmaker God, creating the world and allowing it to tick along on its own. We do not have a puppet-master God, who pulls the strings for entertainment. Rather, in Christ's broken body, we have a God whose passion and compassion allow him to enter into the sorrows of history with us. With this embodied presence, God can say that no matter what you are going through—death, sickness, betrayal—you will not be alone in it. Your pain, heartache, and hope will be shared, for God has walked before us and surrounds us with love.

For Reflection

Think of a time when you went through something difficult—a death, a divorce, an illness. Write it down. Was there a particular person who had gone through a similar situation and understood what you were going through? How did they comfort you?

"All Shall Be Well" Is Anchored in Creation

And in these same five words, said before, "I may make all things well," I understand powerful consolation from all the deeds of our Lord which are still to be performed; for just as the blessed Trinity created everything from nothing, just so the same blessed Trinity will make well all things which are not well.

I have a temporary home in the country, where a window looks out on a patch of land. Each day I look beyond that glass, startled by creation. The chipmunks chase one another, the bunnies chew on bits of greenery, while birds vie for the best spot on the feeder. It does not take long with these creatures before the stress of my day melts away and I'm ushered into a different reality. I breathe deeply and know that all shall be well.

Creation surrounds us, making us understand that even when there seems to be no way out of our anxiety, God can make a way. Even when life feels unmanageable, we can count on the sun coming up each morning and the stars glistening at night. We know that we have the ground beneath us, supporting and sustaining us. The breath we inhale gives us life.

In other words, we can understand that just as God formed the creatures of the earth, the fish of the sea, and the birds of the air, God can make all things well.

For Reflection

Take a walk, if you are able. As you walk, listen for the birds singing over your head. Try to spot as many nonhuman creatures as you can. As you watch them, notice how God provides for them. Remind yourself that God will provide for you too.

Nurturing Contentment

I understand this in two ways: one is that I am well content that I do not know it; and the other is that I am glad and joyful because I shall know it.

Countless studies have been done on how people survive tough situations. Researchers try to figure out why certain people have resilience or contentment in difficult situations. One thing they have discovered is that people who go into a situation understanding that the best outcome will occur are the ones who have the most resilience.

I think of Julian's life, how the death toll rose around her, how she herself lay at death's door, yet she still understood that truth: "All is well."

How could that be? It was the case because Julian knew that the things that were not well would be well. She was content in all that she had in the present moment, and when she wasn't, she held fast to the hope of what would come.

It is a powerful orientation toward life, to understand that all will be well. That the God of the hazelnut and the universe is for you, rooting for you, and wanting the best for your life.

For Reflection

In what areas of your life are you content? In what areas are you seeking contentment? Can you trust that all things will be well in those too?

Conditions in Those Who Pray

I saw two conditions in those who pray, according to what I have felt myself. One is that they will not pray for anything at all but for the thing which is God's will and to his glory; another is that they apply themselves always and with all their might to entreat the thing which is his will and to his glory.

Our family attended a silent auction for my daughter's elementary school. Scanning the prizes, I realized there were more items stuffed into one basket than my daughter had gotten in a lifetime of Christmases.

I spotted a boy on the side of the room, praying with the earnestness of Job. He wanted to win a basket so badly that he was asking God for divine intervention on the matter.

My heart sank, as chances held that the boy would not have a basket at the end of the day. I longed to tell him not to give up on God or on prayer, even though prayer doesn't exactly work that way. God is not our personal genie who does our bidding when we rub the supplication bottle.

Don't get me wrong. God wants to hear our hopes and dreams (even if they are material in nature). Yet, as a person becomes prayerful, their perspective shifts. They begin to see how God's will outshines their personal desires and limited perspective. Even when prayer may not change our conditions, it changes us. For Julian, prayer creates a unity and friendship with God such that God's will becomes our only desire.

For Reflection

Sit down with a journal or a piece of paper. Breathe deeply and listen for God. Then write down how you think your perspective has shifted.

Barren and Dry

But still in all this, often our trust is not complete, for we are not certain that almighty God hears us, because of our unworthiness, it seems to us, and because we are feeling nothing at all; for often we are as barren and dry after our prayers as we were before.

I can easily point to the barren days of my life. I recall when a much-longed-for pregnancy ended abruptly. I remember the seemingly endless days before a loved one died, and I yearned, simultaneously, for more sweet moments of their company *and* for their suffering to end in peace. I walk through days of pleading with God, praying that I'm happy to do God's will if I only knew what that was. In these moments, I cry out but hear no answer. I sit in an open posture, ready to receive the Spirit's wisdom, but I find myself in the tiny echo chamber of my own thoughts.

I take comfort in knowing I am not alone in these barren days. For God whispers in Julian's ear, revealing visions as small as a hazelnut and as large as the universe. Yet, Julian speaks of times when her thirst for God is not quenched, when her longings are not satiated. I feel closer to Julian with these confessions, this realization that I am not alone, even in my solitude.

For Reflection

Søren Kierkegaard says that life must be lived forward but can only be understood backward. Write down a barren time in your life. How do you understand that time now? Did you gain wisdom from the solitude?

Prayer Unites the Soul to God

Prayer unites the soul to God, for although the soul may always be like God in nature and substance, it is often unlike him in condition through human sin.

If we are very lucky, we can unite our soul with some-one else. Through art, singing, or love, we experience that moment when our own emotions, tune, and plea-sure merge in order to create a bond with another. We look at a painting and we allow it to stir a mood within us. With song, a connection forges when we sing in the same melody. In our relationships, our affection grows beyond self-indulgent pleasure into a simple longing for the other person's presence and well-being.

In the same way, prayer unites the soul to God. In prayer, we may start out seeking a particular outcome, but then we slowly surrender our understandings to God's wisdom. We might begin to see the world and the people around us as serving our own needs, but then we let go of our grasping and open ourselves to new possibilities beyond what we could ask or imag-ine. It is not a sacrifice of the self, but an intensity of a self that shines with meaning and purpose. And slowly, we become united to God's way.

For Reflection

When have you felt most connected with God? Name a place, time, or experience that made you feel that particular unity.

Sin Has No Ontology

O, wretched sin, what are you? You are nothing. For I saw that God is in everything; I did not see you. And when I saw that God has made everything, I did not see you. And when I saw that God is in everything, I did not see you. And when I saw that God does everything that is done, the less and the greater, I did not see you.

Many theologians speak of the flesh and the spirit as being at war with one another, because they adhere to an idea that the flesh is bad and the spirit is good. This idea goes against the truth of creation. For when God creates us from the dust of the earth and blows life into us, God declares that we are good, made in the image of God.

In its extreme, the idea that the flesh is bad can become dangerous. When we see our own flesh as evil, then we can begin to think that others are evil as well. In the United States, we have a history of abused children, whipped slaves, and tortured prisoners that came out of the idea that we can beat flesh into submission.

Julian provides an antidote to this poisonous theology. She says that sin is not created by God. It is nothing. Sin is not our flesh or our being, but it is the thing that destroys our flesh or our being. Our flesh and spirit interconnect so that when we take care of our flesh, our spirits flourish.

For Reflection

What is something you can do today to take care of your flesh? Are you hungry, anxious, or tired? Do you need rest or food, exercise or water? Do what you can to care for your body, remembering that it is God's good creation.

Sin Annihilates

And so I am certain that you are nothing, and all those who love you and delight you and follow you and deliberately end in you, I am sure that they will be brought to nothing with you and eternally confounded.

Headache and nausea greet us after a night of binging. Tears follow empty sex. Guilt floods after an unfaithful relationship. Stomach acid flows when we betray a friend. Hunger grows when we consume with a ravenous greed.

Sin can lead us to a certain annihilation in so many ways. And when we follow the path of nothing, then we are brought to nothing. We break the bonds of our relationships, we break the promises that we made to ourselves, and we are left with only our own destruction.

I cannot think of a worse fate than the annihilation of the soul: to imagine a path that leads only to the destruction of love and peace, that leaves us only with the wretched grasping and furious hitting.

For Reflection

Write down the things that give you abundant life right now—the relationships, people, places, feelings, passions, tastes, and smells. What can you do to nurture these things?

What Divides Us?

What is everything on earth that divides us? I answer and say that in the respect in which it serves us it is good, and in the respect in which it will perish it is wretchedness, and in the respect that a man sets his heart upon it otherwise than thus it is sin.

Each time Barbara went into the office, she had to put her mask on. It wasn't an actual mask but an invisible one, like an actor walking on stage to perform an ancient Greek play. When she slipped it on, she became another person—someone who was tough and ruthless. Barbara felt like she had to overcome her natural vulnerabilities and emotional tenderness in order to work in her office. However, the longer she worked there, the more her life felt divided. The work that she did was not always ethical, and when she began struggling with certain moral issues, she put on the mask. She felt separated from her authentic self, and it wasn't long before she felt separated from God.

Throughout Julian's life, she seeks unity. She longs for our souls to be united with God, yet she understands that most of us live a divided life in one way or another. We wear masks that separate us from God and from ourselves.

For Reflection

Where are the fractures in your life? Where do you feel divided? Is there a place where you do not feel like you can be your authentic self? What changes can you make to live a more united life?

Confidence in God's Love

For all the attributes of the blessed Trinity, it is God's will that we have most confidence in his delight and his love.

It had been years since the divorce, but Christy could not help but remember all the things she had done wrong. She thought of the heated words, the bitter betrayals, and the overwhelming greed. She worried about her child and how the nightmare situation affected him. She had gotten to the place of forgiving her husband and their friends. But there was still one strand of resentment that she held too tightly—she could not forgive herself. She ruminated on all the ways she had messed up, how she could have said things better, and how things might have turned out differently.

Though this thinking lured Christy more and more into depression, she knew that God wanted something better for her. God longed for her to forget her sins and doubtful fears.

Finally, Christy began to listen to all the pain she held inside. Listening to herself, she had a new compassion for her past. She learned from God's courtesy. And slowly, as she lived into God's grace, she finally began to find some grace for herself.

For Reflection

What does it mean that God wants us to forget our sin and fears? Is there a particular sin you are holding on to now? Can you extend God's great courtesy to yourself?

God's Desire

God wants us to always be strong in our love, and peaceful and restful as he is towards us, and we want us to be, for ourselves and for our fellow Christians, what he is for us.

There is a simple psychological truth that sprang up with the writings of Karen Horney—that in order to love one another, we must learn to love ourselves. The psychology has become a part of our mainstream thought, but too often we do not practice it as Christians.

Yet, the words of Julian ring true. As we grow in our understanding of God's love for us, we will know God's peace and rest. And out of that abundance of the soul, we will begin to treat ourselves with peace and love. And when all of that is bubbling up in our souls, then it will begin to overflow in our relationships with our family, friends, and neighbors.

That is what Julian leaves with us—a sure sense of God's love, peace, and rest.

For Reflection

Have you taken time to rest this week? Put "Rest" in your calendar right now and be sure you make space to delight in God's presence and love.

Held in God's Comfort

For it is God's will that we do all in our power to preserve our consolation, for bliss lasts forevermore, and pain is passing, and will be reduced to nothing for those who will be saved. Therefore it is not God's will that when we feel pain we should pursue it in sorrow and mourning for it, but that suddenly we should pass it over, and preserve ourselves in the endless delight which is God.

Great comfort awaits a child with a skinned knee when he crawls into his mother's lap. Then, with tears in his eyes, he presents the stinging pain to her as he folds himself into the warmth of her embrace. In that space, healing begins. Within her arms, the boy knows that no pain can be greater than his mother's love. Even when the wound radiates with burning heat, when he feels the embarrassment from the other children laughing at his fall, or when it turns out he lost the game with the tumble—all of that sorrow is held as she surrounds it and contains it. As his mother strokes his hair and murmurs her empathy, he knows that all of his wounds can rest there, in her love.

The child learns, from those early experiences, the great truth of Julian of Norwich's words: that we are held in God's comfort. For when we wake up to the awareness of God's loving arms surrounding us, then we can present our wounds to God, rest in loving care, and find comfort in endless enjoyment.

For Reflection

Meditate on the word *embrace*. Then write down the thoughts that occurred to you.

Passages

All excerpts come from *Julian of Norwich: Showings*, translated and introduced by Edmund Colledge, OSA, and James Walsh, SJ, copyright © 1978 by Paulist Press, Inc. Page numbers for each excerpt are given below.

Day 21: 157
Day 22: 158
Day 23: 166
Day 24: 166
Day 25: 167
Day 26: 167
Day 27: 168
Day 28: 168
Day 29: 170
Day 30: 205